Gift Giving In A Snap!

Stephanie Hoover

Saphire Publishing
PO Box 695
Alturas, CA 96101

Copyright © 2013 Stephanie Hoover

ISBN: 1494714582
ISBN-13: 978-1494714581

Printed in the United States for Saphire Publishing.

Saphire Publishing
PO Box 695
Alturas, CA 96101

INTRODUCTION

When I was young, I had created a booklet similar to this, to make
my life easier. Of course, back then, it was pages stapled together.
But as I was thinking about those days, I thought, "Wouldn't it be
nice to make this available for everybody?" So here it is. Use each
page for a friend or relative, that you might want to send a card or
gift to, for any occasion. Then, whenever someone comments
about something they need, want or like, write it down. Then you
never have to worry about remembering what to get people, at the
last minute.

INDEX OF NAMES

1. _____
2. _____
3. _____
4. _____
5. _____
6. _____
7. _____
8. _____
9. _____
10. _____
11. _____
12. _____
13. _____
14. _____
15. _____
16. _____
17. _____
18. _____
19. _____
20. _____
21. _____
22. _____

INDEX OF NAMES

23. _____
24. _____
25. _____
26. _____
27. _____
28. _____
29. _____
30. _____
31. _____
32. _____
33. _____
34. _____
35. _____
36. _____
37. _____
38. _____
39. _____
40. _____
41. _____
42. _____
43. _____
44. _____

INDEX OF NAMES

45. _____

46. _____

47. _____

48. _____

49. _____

50. _____

51. _____

52. _____

53. _____

54. _____

55. _____

56. _____

57. _____

58. _____

59. _____

60. _____

61. _____

62. _____

63. _____

64. _____

65. _____

66. _____

INDEX OF NAMES

67. _____

68. _____

69. _____

70. _____

71. _____

72. _____

73. _____

74. _____

75. _____

76. _____

77. _____

78. _____

79. _____

80. _____

81. _____

82. _____

83. _____

84. _____

85. _____

86. _____

87. _____

88. _____

Name: _____

Address: _____

_____

Phone: _____

Birthdate: _____

Favorite Colors:_____

Favorite Characters:_____

Collections:_____

_____

Need:_____

_____

_____

_____

_____

_____

_____

Wants:_____

_____

_____

_____

_____

_____

_____

Name: _____

Address: _____

_____

Phone: _____

Birthdate: _____

Favorite Colors: _____

Favorite Characters: _____

Collections: _____

_____

Need: _____

_____

_____

_____

_____

_____

Wants: _____

_____

_____

_____

_____

_____

Name: _____
Address: _____
_____
Phone: _____
Birthdate: _____

Favorite Colors:_____
Favorite Characters:_____
Collections:_____
_____

Need:_____
_____
_____
_____
_____
_____
_____
_____

Wants:_____
_____
_____
_____
_____
_____
_____

Name: _____

Address: _____

_____

Phone: _____

Birthdate: _____

Favorite Colors: _____

Favorite Characters: _____

Collections: _____

_____

Need: _____

_____

_____

_____

_____

_____

Wants: _____

_____

_____

_____

_____

_____

Name: _____

Address: _____

_____

Phone: _____

Birthdate: _____

Favorite Colors: _____

Favorite Characters: _____

Collections: _____

_____

Need: _____

_____

_____

_____

_____

_____

_____

Wants: _____

_____

_____

_____

_____

_____

_____

Name: _____

Address: _____

_____

Phone: _____

Birthdate: _____

Favorite Colors:_____

Favorite Characters:_____

Collections:_____

_____

Need:_____

_____

_____

_____

_____

_____

_____

Wants:_____

_____

_____

_____

_____

_____

_____

Name: _____

Address: _____
_____

Phone: _____

Birthdate: _____

Favorite Colors:_____

Favorite Characters:_____

Collections:_____

_____

Need:_____

_____

_____

_____

_____

_____

Wants:_____

_____

_____

_____

_____

_____

Name: _____

Address: _____

_____

Phone: _____

Birthdate: _____

Favorite Colors:_____

Favorite Characters:_____

Collections:_____

_____

Need:_____

_____

_____

_____

_____

_____

_____

Wants:_____

_____

_____

_____

_____

_____

_____

Name: _____

Address: _____

_____

Phone: _____

Birthdate: _____

Favorite Colors:_____

Favorite Characters:_____

Collections:_____

_____

Need:_____

_____

_____

_____

_____

_____

_____

Wants:_____

_____

_____

_____

_____

_____

_____

Name: _____

Address: _____

_____

Phone: _____

Birthdate: _____

Favorite Colors: _____

Favorite Characters: _____

Collections: _____

_____

Need: _____

_____

_____

_____

_____

Wants: _____

_____

_____

_____

_____

_____

Name: _____

Address: _____

_____

Phone: _____

Birthdate: _____

Favorite Colors:_____

Favorite Characters:_____

Collections:_____

_____

Need:_____

_____

_____

_____

_____

_____

_____

Wants:_____

_____

_____

_____

_____

_____

_____

Name: _____

Address: _____

_____

Phone: _____

Birthdate: _____

Favorite Colors:_____

Favorite Characters:_____

Collections:_____

_____

Need:_____

_____

_____

_____

_____

_____

_____

Wants:_____

_____

_____

_____

_____

_____

_____

Name: _____

Address: _____

_____

Phone: _____

Birthdate: _____

Favorite Colors:_____

Favorite Characters:_____

Collections:_____

_____

Need:_____

_____

_____

_____

_____

_____

Wants:_____

_____

_____

_____

_____

_____

Name: _____

Address: _____

_____

Phone: _____

Birthdate: _____

Favorite Colors: _____

Favorite Characters: _____

Collections: _____

_____

Need: _____

_____

_____

_____

_____

_____

_____

Wants: _____

_____

_____

_____

_____

_____

_____

Name: _____

Address: _____

_____

Phone: _____

Birthdate: _____

Favorite Colors: _____

Favorite Characters: _____

Collections: _____

_____

Need: _____

_____

_____

_____

_____

_____

_____

Wants: _____

_____

_____

_____

_____

_____

_____

Name: _____

Address: _____

_____

Phone: _____

Birthdate: _____

Favorite Colors: _____

Favorite Characters: _____

Collections: _____

_____

Need: _____

_____

_____

_____

_____

_____

_____

Wants: _____

_____

_____

_____

_____

_____

_____

Name: _____

Address: _____
_____

Phone: _____

Birthdate: _____

Favorite Colors:_____

Favorite Characters:_____

Collections:_____
_____

Need:_____
_____
_____
_____
_____
_____
_____

Wants:_____
_____
_____
_____
_____
_____
_____

Name: _____

Address: _____

_____

Phone: _____

Birthdate: _____

Favorite Colors: _____

Favorite Characters: _____

Collections: _____

_____

Need: _____

_____

_____

_____

_____

_____

_____

Wants: _____

_____

_____

_____

_____

_____

Name: _____

Address: _____

_____

Phone: _____

Birthdate: _____

Favorite Colors:_____

Favorite Characters:_____

Collections:_____

_____

Need:_____

_____

_____

_____

_____

_____

_____

Wants:_____

_____

_____

_____

_____

_____

_____

Name: _____

Address: _____

_____

Phone: _____

Birthdate: _____

Favorite Colors: _____

Favorite Characters: _____

Collections: _____

_____

Need: _____

_____

_____

_____

_____

_____

_____

Wants: _____

_____

_____

_____

_____

_____

_____

Name: _____

Address: _____

_____

Phone: _____

Birthdate: _____

Favorite Colors:_____

Favorite Characters:_____

Collections:_____

_____

Need:_____

_____

_____

_____

_____

Wants:_____

_____

_____

_____

_____

Name: _____

Address: _____
_____

Phone: _____

Birthdate: _____

Favorite Colors: _____

Favorite Characters: _____

Collections: _____
_____

Need: _____
_____
_____
_____
_____
_____
_____

Wants: _____
_____
_____
_____
_____
_____
_____

Name: _____

Address: _____

_____

Phone: _____

Birthdate: _____

Favorite Colors:_____

Favorite Characters:_____

Collections:_____

_____

Need:_____

_____

_____

_____

_____

_____

_____

Wants:_____

_____

_____

_____

_____

_____

_____

Name: _____

Address: _____

_____

Phone: _____

Birthdate: _____

Favorite Colors: _____

Favorite Characters: _____

Collections: _____

_____

Need: _____

_____

_____

_____

_____

_____

_____

Wants: _____

_____

_____

_____

_____

_____

Name: _____

Address: _____

_____

Phone: _____

Birthdate: _____

Favorite Colors: _____

Favorite Characters: _____

Collections: _____

_____

Need: _____

_____

_____

_____

_____

_____

_____

Wants: _____

_____

_____

_____

_____

_____

_____

Name: _____

Address: _____

_____

Phone: _____

Birthdate: _____

Favorite Colors:_____

Favorite Characters:_____

Collections:_____

_____

Need:_____

_____

_____

_____

_____

_____

_____

Wants:_____

_____

_____

_____

_____

_____

Name: _____
Address: _____
_____
Phone: _____
Birthdate: _____

Favorite Colors: _____
Favorite Characters: _____
Collections: _____
_____

Need: _____
_____
_____
_____
_____
_____
_____

Wants: _____
_____
_____
_____
_____
_____
_____

Name: _____

Address: _____

_____

Phone: _____

Birthdate: _____

Favorite Colors:_____

Favorite Characters:_____

Collections:_____

_____

Need:_____

_____

_____

_____

_____

_____

_____

Wants:_____

_____

_____

_____

_____

_____

_____

Name: _____

Address: _____

_____

Phone: _____

Birthdate: _____

Favorite Colors:_____

Favorite Characters:_____

Collections:_____

_____

Need:_____

_____

_____

_____

_____

_____

_____

Wants:_____

_____

_____

_____

_____

_____

_____

Name: _____

Address: _____

_____

Phone: _____

Birthdate: _____

Favorite Colors:_____

Favorite Characters:_____

Collections:_____

_____

Need:_____

_____

_____

_____

_____

_____

Wants:_____

_____

_____

_____

_____

_____

Name: _____
Address: _____
_____
Phone: _____
Birthdate: _____

Favorite Colors:_____
Favorite Characters:_____
Collections:_____
_____

Need:_____
_____
_____
_____
_____
_____
_____

Wants:_____
_____
_____
_____
_____
_____
_____

Name: _____

Address: _____

_____

Phone: _____

Birthdate: _____

Favorite Colors:_____

Favorite Characters:_____

Collections:_____

_____

Need:_____

_____

_____

_____

_____

_____

_____

Wants:_____

_____

_____

_____

_____

_____

Name: _____

Address: _____

_____

Phone: _____

Birthdate: _____

Favorite Colors:_____

Favorite Characters:_____

Collections:_____

_____

Need:_____

_____

_____

_____

_____

_____

_____

Wants:_____

_____

_____

_____

_____

_____

_____

Name: _____

Address: _____
_____

Phone: _____

Birthdate: _____

Favorite Colors: _____

Favorite Characters: _____

Collections: _____
_____

Need: _____
_____
_____
_____
_____
_____
_____

Wants: _____
_____
_____
_____
_____
_____
_____

Name: _____

Address: _____

_____

Phone: _____

Birthdate: _____

Favorite Colors: _____

Favorite Characters: _____

Collections: _____

_____

Need: _____

_____

_____

_____

_____

_____

Wants: _____

_____

_____

_____

_____

_____

Name: _____

Address: _____

_____

Phone: _____

Birthdate: _____

Favorite Colors: _____

Favorite Characters: _____

Collections:_____

_____

Need:_____

_____

_____

_____

_____

_____

_____

_____

Wants:_____

_____

_____

_____

_____

_____

_____

_____

Name: _____

Address: _____

_____

Phone: _____

Birthdate: _____

Favorite Colors: _____

Favorite Characters: _____

Collections: _____

_____

Need: _____

_____

_____

_____

_____

_____

_____

Wants: _____

_____

_____

_____

_____

_____

_____

Name: _____

Address: _____

_____

Phone: _____

Birthdate: _____

Favorite Colors:_____

Favorite Characters:_____

Collections:_____

_____

Need:_____

_____

_____

_____

_____

_____

_____

Wants:_____

_____

_____

_____

_____

_____

_____

Name: _____

Address: _____

_____

Phone: _____

Birthdate: _____

Favorite Colors: _____

Favorite Characters: _____

Collections: _____

_____

Need: _____

_____

_____

_____

_____

_____

_____

Wants: _____

_____

_____

_____

_____

_____

_____

Name: _____

Address: _____

_____

Phone: _____

Birthdate: _____

Favorite Colors:_____

Favorite Characters:_____

Collections:_____

_____

Need:_____

_____

_____

_____

_____

_____

_____

Wants:_____

_____

_____

_____

_____

_____

Name: _____

Address: _____

_____

Phone: _____

Birthdate: _____

Favorite Colors:_____

Favorite Characters:_____

Collections:_____

_____

Need:_____

_____

_____

_____

_____

_____

_____

Wants:_____

_____

_____

_____

_____

_____

_____

Name: _____

Address: _____

_____

Phone: _____

Birthdate: _____

Favorite Colors: _____

Favorite Characters: _____

Collections: _____

_____

Need: _____

_____

_____

_____

_____

_____

_____

Wants: _____

_____

_____

_____

_____

_____

_____

Name: _____

Address: _____

_____

Phone: _____

Birthdate: _____

Favorite Colors:_____

Favorite Characters:_____

Collections:_____

_____

Need:_____

_____

_____

_____

_____

_____

_____

Wants:_____

_____

_____

_____

_____

_____

Name: _____

Address: _____

_____

Phone: _____

Birthdate: _____

Favorite Colors:_____

Favorite Characters:_____

Collections:_____

_____

Need:_____

_____

_____

_____

_____

_____

_____

Wants:_____

_____

_____

_____

_____

_____

_____

Name: _____

Address: _____

_____

Phone: _____

Birthdate: _____

Favorite Colors:_____

Favorite Characters:_____

Collections:_____

_____

Need:_____

_____

_____

_____

_____

_____

_____

Wants:_____

_____

_____

_____

_____

_____

_____

Name: _____

Address: _____

_____

Phone: _____

Birthdate: _____

Favorite Colors:_____

Favorite Characters:_____

Collections:_____

_____

Need:_____

_____

_____

_____

_____

_____

Wants:_____

_____

_____

_____

_____

_____

Name: _____

Address: _____

_____

Phone: _____

Birthdate: _____

Favorite Colors:_____

Favorite Characters:_____

Collections:_____

_____

Need:_____

_____

_____

_____

_____

_____

_____

Wants:_____

_____

_____

_____

_____

_____

_____

Name: _____

Address: _____

_____

Phone: _____

Birthdate: _____

Favorite Colors:_____

Favorite Characters:_____

Collections:_____

_____

Need:_____

_____

_____

_____

_____

_____

Wants:_____

_____

_____

_____

_____

_____

_____

Name: _____

Address: _____
_____

Phone: _____

Birthdate: _____

Favorite Colors: _____

Favorite Characters: _____

Collections: _____
_____

Need: _____
_____
_____
_____
_____
_____

Wants: _____
_____
_____
_____
_____
_____

Name: _____

Address: _____

_____

Phone: _____

Birthdate: _____

Favorite Colors:_____

Favorite Characters:_____

Collections:_____

_____

Need:_____

_____

_____

_____

_____

_____

_____

Wants:_____

_____

_____

_____

_____

_____

_____

Name: _____

Address: _____

_____

Phone: _____

Birthdate: _____

Favorite Colors:_____

Favorite Characters:_____

Collections:_____

_____

Need:_____

_____

_____

_____

_____

_____

_____

Wants:_____

_____

_____

_____

_____

_____

Name: _____

Address: _____

_____

Phone: _____

Birthdate: _____

Favorite Colors: _____

Favorite Characters: _____

Collections: _____

_____

Need: _____

_____

_____

_____

_____

_____

_____

Wants: _____

_____

_____

_____

_____

_____

_____

Name: _____

Address: _____

_____

Phone: _____

Birthdate: _____

Favorite Colors:_____

Favorite Characters:_____

Collections:_____

_____

Need:_____

_____

_____

_____

_____

_____

_____

Wants:_____

_____

_____

_____

_____

_____

_____

```
Name: _____
Address: _____
_____
Phone: _____
Birthdate: _____

Favorite Colors:_____
Favorite Characters:_____
Collections:_____
_____

Need:_____
_____
_____
_____
_____
_____

Wants:_____
_____
_____
_____
_____
_____
```

Name: _____

Address: _____
_____

Phone: _____

Birthdate: _____

Favorite Colors:_____

Favorite Characters:_____

Collections:_____
_____

Need:_____
_____
_____
_____
_____
_____
_____

Wants:_____
_____
_____
_____
_____
_____
_____

Name: _____

Address: _____

_____

Phone: _____

Birthdate: _____

Favorite Colors:_____

Favorite Characters:_____

Collections:_____

_____

Need:_____

_____

_____

_____

_____

_____

_____

Wants:_____

_____

_____

_____

_____

_____

_____

Name: _____

Address: _____
_____

Phone: _____

Birthdate: _____

Favorite Colors:_____

Favorite Characters:_____

Collections:_____
_____

Need:_____
_____
_____
_____
_____
_____
_____

Wants:_____
_____
_____
_____
_____
_____

Name: _____

Address: _____
_____

Phone: _____

Birthdate: _____

Favorite Colors: _____

Favorite Characters: _____

Collections: _____
_____

Need: _____
_____
_____
_____
_____
_____
_____

Wants: _____
_____
_____
_____
_____
_____
_____

Name: _____

Address: _____

_____

Phone: _____

Birthdate: _____

Favorite Colors: _____

Favorite Characters: _____

Collections: _____

_____

Need: _____

_____

_____

_____

_____

_____

Wants: _____

_____

_____

_____

_____

_____

_____

Name: _____

Address: _____

_____

Phone: _____

Birthdate: _____

Favorite Colors:_____

Favorite Characters:_____

Collections:_____

_____

Need:_____

_____

_____

_____

_____

_____

_____

Wants:_____

_____

_____

_____

_____

_____

_____

Name: _____

Address: _____

_____

Phone: _____

Birthdate: _____

Favorite Colors:_____

Favorite Characters:_____

Collections:_____

_____

Need:_____

_____

_____

_____

_____

_____

_____

Wants:_____

_____

_____

_____

_____

_____

Name: _____
Address: _____
_____
Phone: _____
Birthdate: _____

Favorite Colors: _____
Favorite Characters: _____
Collections: _____
_____

Need: _____
_____
_____
_____
_____
_____

Wants: _____
_____
_____
_____
_____
_____

Name: _____

Address: _____

_____

Phone: _____

Birthdate: _____

Favorite Colors: _____

Favorite Characters: _____

Collections: _____

_____

Need: _____

_____

_____

_____

_____

_____

_____

Wants: _____

_____

_____

_____

_____

_____

_____

Name: _____

Address: _____

_____

Phone: _____

Birthdate: _____

Favorite Colors: _____

Favorite Characters: _____

Collections: _____

_____

Need: _____

_____

_____

_____

_____

_____

_____

Wants: _____

_____

_____

_____

_____

_____

_____

Name: _____

Address: _____
_____

Phone: _____

Birthdate: _____

Favorite Colors: _____

Favorite Characters:_____

Collections:_____
_____

Need:_____
_____
_____
_____
_____
_____

Wants:_____
_____
_____
_____
_____

Name: _____

Address: _____

_____

Phone: _____

Birthdate: _____

Favorite Colors:_____

Favorite Characters:_____

Collections:_____

_____

Need:_____

_____

_____

_____

_____

_____

_____

Wants:_____

_____

_____

_____

_____

_____

_____

Name: _____

Address: _____

_____

Phone: _____

Birthdate: _____

Favorite Colors: _____

Favorite Characters: _____

Collections: _____

_____

Need: _____

_____

_____

_____

_____

_____

_____

Wants: _____

_____

_____

_____

_____

_____

_____

Name: _____

Address: _____

_____

Phone: _____

Birthdate: _____

Favorite Colors:_____

Favorite Characters:_____

Collections:_____

_____

Need:_____

_____

_____

_____

_____

_____

Wants:_____

_____

_____

_____

_____

_____

Name: _____

Address: _____

_____

Phone: _____

Birthdate: _____

Favorite Colors: _____

Favorite Characters: _____

Collections: _____

_____

Need: _____

_____

_____

_____

_____

_____

_____

Wants: _____

_____

_____

_____

_____

_____

_____

Name: _____
Address: _____
_____
Phone: _____
Birthdate: _____

Favorite Colors:_____
Favorite Characters:_____
Collections:_____
_____

Need:_____
_____
_____
_____
_____
_____

Wants:_____
_____
_____
_____
_____
_____

Name: _____

Address: _____
_____

Phone: _____

Birthdate: _____

Favorite Colors:_____

Favorite Characters:_____

Collections:_____
_____

Need:_____
_____
_____
_____
_____
_____
_____

Wants:_____
_____
_____
_____
_____
_____
_____

Name: _____

Address: _____
_____
Phone: _____
Birthdate: _____

Favorite Colors:_____
Favorite Characters:_____
Collections:_____
_____

Need:_____
_____
_____
_____
_____
_____
_____

Wants:_____
_____
_____
_____
_____
_____
_____

Name: _____

Address: _____

_____

Phone: _____

Birthdate: _____

Favorite Colors:_____

Favorite Characters:_____

Collections:_____

_____

Need:_____

_____

_____

_____

_____

_____

Wants:_____

_____

_____

_____

_____

_____

Name: _____

Address: _____

_____

Phone: _____

Birthdate: _____

Favorite Colors: _____

Favorite Characters: _____

Collections: _____

_____

Need: _____

_____

_____

_____

_____

_____

_____

Wants: _____

_____

_____

_____

_____

_____

_____

Name: _____

Address: _____

_____

Phone: _____

Birthdate: _____

Favorite Colors:_____

Favorite Characters:_____

Collections:_____

_____

Need:_____

_____

_____

_____

_____

_____

_____

Wants:_____

_____

_____

_____

_____

_____

_____

Name: _____

Address: _____

_____

Phone: _____

Birthdate: _____

Favorite Colors:_____

Favorite Characters:_____

Collections:_____

_____

Need:_____

_____

_____

_____

_____

_____

Wants:_____

_____

_____

_____

_____

_____

Name: _____

Address: _____

_____

Phone: _____

Birthdate: _____

Favorite Colors:_____

Favorite Characters:_____

Collections:_____

_____

Need:_____

_____

_____

_____

_____

_____

_____

Wants:_____

_____

_____

_____

_____

_____

_____

Name: _____

Address: _____

_____

Phone: _____

Birthdate: _____

Favorite Colors:_____

Favorite Characters:_____

Collections:_____

_____

Need:_____

_____

_____

_____

_____

_____

Wants:_____

_____

_____

_____

_____

_____

_____

Name: _____

Address: _____

_____

Phone: _____

Birthdate: _____

Favorite Colors:_____

Favorite Characters:_____

Collections:_____

_____

Need:_____

_____

_____

_____

_____

_____

Wants:_____

_____

_____

_____

_____

_____

Name: _____
Address: _____
_____
Phone: _____
Birthdate: _____

Favorite Colors: _____
Favorite Characters: _____
Collections: _____
_____

Need: _____
_____
_____
_____
_____
_____
_____

Wants: _____
_____
_____
_____
_____
_____
_____

Name: _____

Address: _____

_____

Phone: _____

Birthdate: _____

Favorite Colors:_____

Favorite Characters:_____

Collections:_____

_____

Need:_____

_____

_____

_____

_____

_____

Wants:_____

_____

_____

_____

_____

_____

_____

Name: _____

Address: _____

_____

Phone: _____

Birthdate: _____

Favorite Colors: _____

Favorite Characters:_____

Collections:_____

_____

Need:_____

_____

_____

_____

_____

_____

_____

Wants:_____

_____

_____

_____

_____

_____

_____

Name: _____

Address: _____

_____

Phone: _____

Birthdate: _____

Favorite Colors:_____

Favorite Characters:_____

Collections:_____

_____

Need:_____

_____

_____

_____

_____

_____

Wants:_____

_____

_____

_____

_____

_____

_____

Name: _____

Address: _____

_____

Phone: _____

Birthdate: _____

Favorite Colors:_____

Favorite Characters:_____

Collections:_____

_____

Need:_____

_____

_____

_____

_____

_____

_____

Wants:_____

_____

_____

_____

_____

_____

_____

Name: _____

Address: _____

_____

Phone: _____

Birthdate: _____

Favorite Colors:_____

Favorite Characters:_____

Collections:_____

_____

Need:_____

_____

_____

_____

_____

_____

_____

Wants:_____

_____

_____

_____

_____

_____

_____

Name: _____

Address: _____

_____

Phone: _____

Birthdate: _____

Favorite Colors:_____

Favorite Characters:_____

Collections:_____

_____

Need:_____

_____

_____

_____

_____

_____

_____

Wants:_____

_____

_____

_____

_____

_____

_____

Name: _____

Address: _____

_____

Phone: _____

Birthdate: _____

Favorite Colors:_____

Favorite Characters:_____

Collections:_____

_____

Need:_____

_____

_____

_____

_____

_____

_____

Wants:_____

_____

_____

_____

_____

_____

Name: _____

Address: _____

_____

Phone: _____

Birthdate: _____

Favorite Colors: _____

Favorite Characters: _____

Collections:_____

_____

Need:_____

_____

_____

_____

_____

_____

Wants:_____

_____

_____

_____

_____

_____

_____